Artists AND THEIR Cats

in their own words

Edited by
Sylvia Moore
&
Cynthia Navaretta

MIDMARCH ARTS PRESS
New York   1990

MIDMARCH ARTS BOOKS

The Lady Architects: Howe, Manning and Almy, 1893-1937
Camera Fiends and Kodak Girls: 50 Selections by and about Women in
Photography 1840-1930
Yesterday and Tomorrow: California Women Artists
No Bluebonnets, No Yellow Roses: Texas Women in the Arts
Pilgrims and Pioneers: New England Women in the Arts
Whole Arts Directory
Women Artists of the World
Voices of Women: 3 critics on 3 poets on 3 heroines
American Women Artists: Works on Paper
Guide to Women's Art Organizations and Directory for the Arts

Library of Congress Catalog Card Number: 90-061443
ISBN: 1-877675-02-4

Copies of this book may be obtained from:
Midmarch Arts Books
Box 3304 Grand Central
New York, NY 10163

front cover drawing: Judy Seigel
back cover: Joan Brown and Donald, *Cat Temple*, 1982;
cover design: Two Lip Art
typographic design: Barbara Bergeron

CONTENTS 🐾

Introduction

It is becoming commonplace to count one's cats as members of the family. Many 1990 census returns listed cats as household members — for example, one named Puss E. Boots; country of origin: Siam. Magazine and newspaper articles frequently contain statements such as this report from the *New York Times*, "Margaret Atwood lives with her companion, Graeme Gibson, their daughter Jess, and two cats named Fluffy and Blackie . . . ." Though no longer worshiped as in ancient Egypt, cats are obviously highly valued today as participants in family life.

Cats, with their fluid grace and elegant proportions, enhanced by intricate patterns and soft textures of fur, have charmed artists through the centuries. Whether as models, mousers, or amiable companions, they have shared artists' studios, lightened artists' lives and made regular appearances in artwork.

Noted artists like Goya have painted and sculpted cats, while others such as Alexandre Steinlen and Peggy Bacon (and some artists included here) have written and illustrated books on cats. Bacon's *Starting From Scratch* (NY: Julian Messner, Inc., 1945), recalls an early memory of a large white cat named Cinders, a "warrior" with ragged ears and battered nose who was her "first hero." Another pet was the haughty hunter Jezebel, "long, black, and slinky." "Nevertheless," says Bacon, "my heart felt well rewarded whenever she allowed me to scratch her under the chin." Bacon eventually discovered "fireside cats, sofa cats, guest room-bed cats, and lap-cats." She loved them all, and recorded their doings with understanding and humor.

Humans, whether or not they are artists, willingly spend time watching cats perform. As Roger A. Caras pointed out in *A Cat is Watching* (NY: Simon & Schuster, 1989), felines also spend time eyeing humans. Since the average person weighs about 20 times as much as a cat and is about 12 times as tall, "no cat in its right mind would not watch us." We can only ponder whether cats, if they could draw and paint, would record our ways.

Here we offer a selection of cats of all ages, colors and sizes, pedigreed and strays, living and deceased. Each is unique; all are beloved. Their assorted owners, a word we use advisedly (for who can truly own a cat?), have provided descriptive statements that reveal the nature of their human/cat relationships. Most are companionable; some are professional as well; a few approach the erotic or the spiritual. The consensus is that every home and studio should have at least one cat.

— Sylvia Moore and Cynthia Navaretta

The Moore cats

The Navaretta cats
The Siamese connection

Sylvia Moore lives near the big cats of the Bronx Zoo with her husband, Rod, and two housepets, Jet and Tiger Lily, both strays. She can't recall a time in her life when there were no cats in her home and hopes such a time never happens.

Cynthia Navaretta lives with a family of cats — some four generations — all Siamese, except for one black cat named Niko, but addressed as Black Cat. The others, aside from Miccio (in honor of the editor's Italian connection) and Musa (named for Mohammed's favorite cat), have descriptive names such as White Foot, Patte Blanche, White Boots, and such, relating to a distinguishing genetic characteristic of one or more white toes.

Ellen Alt

Sylphide and I shared a studio in Buffalo, New York, where we would often work late into the night. She was a prima donna and had few friends. I was one of them. Sometimes she would reminisce about her glory days at the ballet. Occasionally she'd let me draw on her head. We got along just fine.

Ellen Alt Granting Wishes

Ellen Alt, a native of Buffalo, received a BFA from Massachusetts College of Art in 1978 and an MA in Studio Art from New York University in 1982. Her collages and mixed-media works on paper have been shown in various one-person and group shows in New York, Buffalo, New Haven and Moscow, USSR.

ANNE ARNOLD 🐾

My favorite cat, Christy, was a black Maine Coon cat. I saw him born. He was the first of his litter, and as I watched him crawl up and attach himself to the nipple I knew I wanted him. He grew up to be a wanderer and explorer, so he was called Christy after Christopher Columbus. He liked to ride on my shoulders and follow me for long walks up the road and through the fields and woods in Maine. He was very verbal with many different meows, and he had a wonderful purr. I miss him.

Anne Arnold with Christy

I have always loved animals, art and nature. I migrate like the birds to Maine in the summer and back to New York City for the winter. I had my first solo exhibition of sculpture in 1960 at the Tanager Gallery and my most recent exhibition in 1988 at the Fischbach Gallery, New York, where I have shown since 1964. I teach sculpture and am currently a professor at Brooklyn College, CUNY.

Anne Arnold, *Christy*, 1987, white pine

NANCY BAREIS ❧

This photograph is a self-portrait of myself and Jessie. He is the oldest and smallest of five household pets. He's very playful and has taught me many tricks.

Nancy Bareis, a graduate of Brooklyn College, resides in Brooklyn, New York with four street cats. She is currently photographing the residents and countryside surrounding a small upstate town. And is always on the lookout for posing cats to photograph.

KERRY BART

Here are two of my favorite, if not the most aloof, models. I've worked with them for years . . . but I still would not call them studio cats. They are just too much a part of life.

Quite often when I see them, they've had a hard, busy day; so we all just loll about on the furniture. It's a great comfort to be able to have enough leisure to gaze into the distance, draw, and just plain relax.

Although I'm always behind on various artistic endeavors, my feline friends inspire me with their casual grace and acceptance of the world around them.

CAROLYN BERRY

The photo of Kitty and myself was taken in 1970 by my oldest daughter, who was ten at the time. My two daughters and I were living in Arcata, California, where we had moved from New Paltz, New York, after I had been accepted in the graduate program. I soon discovered that no woman had ever succeeded in getting a Fine Arts masters there (this was 1969-71), and rather than relocate the girls again, I switched to special education. Kitty appeared outside our back door one day. We started feeding him and soon had a friend. Intelligent and funny, a large, beautiful Manx with a tail, he never hunted, but played hide-and-seek with my daughters, running down the hall, doubling back and jumping into a closet or hiding behind a half-open door, then streaking off to another room. He was a welcome addition to the household and studio. I was a single parent then, working part-time and going to school. The cat helped to bond us to a new area and gave the children a replacement for the dog they'd left behind. As a pet, he was infinitely superior to the guinea pigs we tried at first. We loved him dearly. I've done a number of pieces having to do with him as a mysterious spirit.

Carolyn Berry was born in Sweet Springs, Missouri in 1930. She received a BA in Painting from the University of Missouri in 1953. Berry lives and works in Monterey, California, where she and her husband are visited daily by a neighborhood dog named Wolf and a black cat, name unknown.

Carolyn Berry and Kitty

Carolyn Berry's hand-painted 1988 Christmas card

DAVID BRICKMAN 🐾

The photographs are of myself with my cat Sam. Sam is a stay-at-home cat — that is his function — although he started out as a stray. If I didn't have Sam to go home to, I probably would stay at the studio all the time. He gives me something else to be responsible to besides my art and my friends. Cats can be very independent, but they don't like to be left alone. Sam needs me. Fortunately, he doesn't need much else. A little food and water satisfies him. Add some sunshine and he gets ecstatic. Sam is easily amused. Just by using a certain tone of voice, I can have him racing around the apartment in excitement. He's stupid, but he's always there — a friend no matter what. Everybody has times when they can use that kind of faithfulness. I guess this is the way Sam is on the dog side of the cat world. Still, he looks exactly like a cat, and sometimes acts like one, too. By the way, he never ever looks at pictures.

David Brickman was born in 1958 in Albany, New York. He earned his BA in Studio Art at Brown University in 1979 and continued his studies in photography at the Visual Studies Workshop Summer Institute, 1981-82. He resides with his cat Sam on top of their darkroom in a converted warehouse in Albany, New York. A Fine Art photographer with numerous awards and exhibition credits, Brickman is currently involved in the production and marketing of his own line of black-and-white postcards and notecards, while continuing to pursue an artistic career.

Sam manages to eke out an existence by occasionally accepting food and medical attention in lieu of royalties for the best-selling cards that bear his frosty likeness.

David Brickman and Sam
(two views)

JOAN BROWN ❦

I love cats and couldn't imagine being without one. I have three: Donald, an eight and a half year-old Abyssinian; Leela, a Burmese who is also eight and a half; and Fran, a three-year-old Calico. I love and enjoy all of them, but Donald and I have had a special bond since he moved in when he was five months old. He is my constant companion when I'm at home. Donald is highly intelligent, clever and witty, very expressive and affectionate (he likes to hold hands) and never fights — he does not even know how to!

Joan Brown lives in San Francisco and has been a professor of art at the University of California, Berkeley since 1974. Her work is included in many major museums, including the Whitney Museum of American Art, New York, the Museum of Fine Arts, Boston, and the San Francisco Museum of Modern Art. She is the recipient of two National Endowment for the Arts Grants and a Guggenheim Fellowship, and is represented by the Frumkin-Adams Gallery, New York.

One of her paintings, Grey Cat with Madrone and Birch Trees, *is included in the Boston Museum's "Cat Collection" and is reproduced in their note cards along with the cat works of other distinguished artists such as Edouard Manet, Hsü Pei-hung, William Morris Hunt, Samuel F. B. Morse and Alexandre Steinlen.*

Joan Brown and Donald

JEANNE NORMAN CHASE

I have two house cats, Siamese, named Dusty and Suki, who have my attention in the evenings when I go home. But my real love is my studio cat, Tasha, a three-year-old Calico. She guards my studio, an old house, two miles from my home. Tasha sits or sleeps on "her chair" while I am painting. The chair is moved to wherever I am working; sometimes she reaches out and touches my arm, which means, "stop painting and pay attention to me for a while." Five minutes is all she needs at a time.

In the morning when I come to work she is waiting at her special place on a cabinet by the door. When I enter she climbs onto my left shoulder and we make the rounds, turning off the night light, opening curtains and such. She talks to me during this "good morning" session — the rest of the day she is silent while I work.

She is my "Ideal Companion."

Jeanne Norman Chase grew up in California and received her BFA from California State University. She moved to Florida in 1963 to join the faculty of the Ringling School of Art and Design in Sarasota, where she continues to teach. Her works have been included in numerous one-person and group shows throughout the United States.

Artist and Her Studio Cat

JUDY CHICAGO 🍎

My husband, Donald Woodman (the photographer who took this picture), and I like nothing better than piling into our bed with all five of our cats. My particular favorite is Sebastian, who spends his days with me in the studio. Recently, Sebastian has developed diabetes and I have to give him shots daily (Donald abhors needles). His illness has taught me that one has to be prepared to take care of all creatures one loves "for better or for worse."

Judy Chicago is an artist, writer and thinker whose work has had a world-wide impact on art and culture. She is best known for The Dinner Party, *a multi-media installation which presents the symbolic history of women in Western Civilization,* The Birth Project *and* Powerplay.

She is presently engaged in the Holocaust Project, *scheduled for exhibition in 1992.*

Chicago is the author of four books: Through the Flower: My Struggle as a Woman Artist; The Dinner Party: A Symbol of Our Heritage; The Dinner Party Needlework; *and* The Birth Project.

"Five Creatures in a Bed with Virginia Woolf Pillow"; clockwise from left:
Judy Chicago, Mully, Veronica, Virginia Woolf, Sebastian and Inka; not pictured is Poppy

NANCY CHUNN
and PAUL MCMAHON 🐾

Billie Blue Cat is the beloved daughter of Nancy and Paul. She is eight years old and still looks like a kitten. She is a Russian Blue. Billie is very playful and so is Paul. In the course of keeping Billie's playtime demands met, Paul has developed a bunch of cat toys. He even went so far as to market one of them, the Mock Mouse. He is currently working on another cat product that will be easier to mass produce.

Paul McMahon

Nancy Chunn and Billie Blue Cat

Nancy Chunn is a painter who shows at the Ronald Feldman Gallery in New York. Paul McMahon is a musician and artist, who was seen on Cinemax in "Mike's Talent Show." He is a regular on CNBC cable network on KTV, a children's show where he is the "Rock 'n Roll Therapist," making up instant songs in response to the kids' problems. Paul received a New Genres Fellowship from the NEA in 1990.

Paul McMahon Holding Billie Blue Cat — No Hands

Nancy Chunn and Billie Blue Cat

Billie Blue Cat

DULCIE DEE

This is my cat Dashiell Dee, named after the famous writer. He's a very smart tiger cat. I've taught him many tricks. He loves to play with an aluminum foil ball and follows me around like a dog. He isn't afraid of New York City traffic and noise, or even flying in a plane! Now he is in Manila with my grandmother, enjoying being a tropical cat. He eats rice and fish and other delicious catch-of-the-day instead of American cat food and loves to talk and chase the birds. He enjoys digging in the garden and climbing roofs. I visit him whenever I can; he still remembers me and wets my bed to tell me he missed me! This cat is always sunbathing and catnapping, but during the evenings he is Captain Dashiell Dee who catches and kills all the roaches and mice. He has even figured out how to open the back door by himself and sneaks out late at night to go star gazing. A most adorable cat and loving as a child. When he isn't busy being the perfect artist's model, Dashiell Dee is working on his first novel. He is always aware of my pen and sketch pad. He snuggles up and poses without a complaint. He knows one day he'll overthrow Morris the Cat with his calm poise and tiger stripes.

Dulcie Dee, a native New Yorker, returned to the Philippines to complete her education, receiving a BFA from the University of the Philippines. She has exhibited internationally and is presently living and working in Australia, preparing for a major exhibition. At her most recent New York exhibition of "Bodyscapes" paintings and drawings, several works, thought to be too suggestive, were censored and removed before the opening. They were eagerly sought out for purchase. Dee supplements her art income as a free-lance graphic designer.

SUE FULLER 🐾

What a lovely being a cat is! Mine has tiny little white eyelashes and such charming accomplishments by which she twists me around her delicate little paw. Who says there is no communication between species? She knows exactly how to rattle the venetian blinds to wake me up or scratch on the painted door or, all else failing, land on the bed by my head and breathe on my face or bite my nose. She knows to sit near the cupboard when she wants her food, or to jump on a chair right under the kitchen table where I'm trimming a roast. She also demands to be brushed every day on my desk, after I've made my bed. Three taps of the brush on the desk brings her up to the chair and then to the desk when I'm ready. She proffers me one side, then automatically turns around for the other. Switching from the metal teeth to the bristle side of the brush, I then give her a facial under the chin then up to the ears, over the whiskers and delicately over the eyes. And don't forget the frontal ruff! A very satisfactory ritual. What a dear warm soft purring friend! Utterly comforting and furry.

A recent note from Sue Fuller adds:

As you know our cat Greyfer died last spring ('89).

Greyfer is the one who used to eat at his own little table I made from a very good wooden box (dovetailed corners) that apricots from Nieman Marcus came in. So his plate wouldn't slip off I put a plate rail around three sides of the top. He sat before it like a gentleman and addressed his dinner. He merely looked up when he wanted another helping. He was a dear cat.

Well schooled at Carnegie Tech and by stalwarts Hans Hoffman, S. W. Hayter, and Josef Albers, I enjoyed a long career as an active artist in New York City, winning honors and placement in museums. Now retired to Southampton to enjoy the company of my cat in peace and quiet.

Greyfer and Ketzeleh

Ketzeleh (l.) and Greyfer (r.) celebrating Christmas dinner
with friends Fox, Possum and Raccoon

Jane Gilmor 🐾

Some years back I entered my cat. Ms. Kitty Glitter, in the Eleventh Annual All-American Glamour Kitty Contest sponsored by a kitty litter manufacturer. For several months prior to the contest I had been constructing clothing pieces for my cat. This was a continuation of my earlier work concerned with spoofing contemporary social and sexual mores using cat imagery. As Ms. Kitty progressed from regional winner to semi-finalist to one of nine national finalists (out of 20,000 entries) she began to receive local and national publicity, as well as numerous prizes — jeweled collars, engraved silver platters, a television set, as well as a year's supply of kitty litter. Finally we were flown, along with our photographer, to the luxurious Hotel Fontainbleau in Miami Beach for a week of competitions. Included in the week's events were a "mousemobile motorcade" through downtown Miami, "The Kitty Fashion Show," "The Kitty Olympics" and the "Coronation" with the same master of ceremonies who officiated at the Miss Universe Pageant. I documented this bizarre homage to neurotic pet owners and America's Cinderella syndrome with video tape, photographs and film. Since the pageant I have created a series of assemblage constructions from Ms. Kitty's souvenirs and prizes, and another series of three-dimensional pieces based on the wardrobe I developed for her prior to and following the contest. There is an intended tongue-in-cheek irreverence in not only the imagery, but also the materials, colors and forms. The humorous and theatrical aspects of the pieces are references to the "staging" of the All-American Glamour Kitty Contest and to the performance nature of the experience itself.

So began a long relationship between my cat masks and me. It has been the focus of my art — concerned with myth and ritual and especially myths about women — since 1976. Last year Ms. Kitty died at the age of 15. I gave a lecture in her honor in Italy while a resident artist there.

Jane Gilmor has collected a clutch of degrees — BS from Iowa State University, MA, MAT and MFA from the Art Institute of Chicago and the University of Iowa. She has been professor of art at Mount Mercy College in Cedar Rapids since 1974. Her work has been included in numerous one-person and group invitational exhibitions throughout the country. Gilmor often uses animal images to parody sex-related roles in contemporary society, as well as the Great Goddess archetype, combining a woman's body with a cat's head. By content and use of materials she attempts to create "a ritualistic ambiance not unlike that of some bizarre roadside shrine." Her shrine and altar installations combine metal repoussé with video, film and photographic documents of the ritual-performance works she has staged in Greece, Turkey and Egypt.

*All-American
Glamour Kitties,*
Temple of Olympian
Zeus, Athens, 1978

*K. Glitter and The
Two-Headed Cat,*
1977

*Anti-Nuclear Dreams:
Edna's Apparition of
Her Greatness,*
Grand Lodge of Iowa,
Cedar Rapids, 1985

23

MELISSA HARRIS ❦

Jupiter is without a doubt my best friend. I think he would say the same about me, though he also loves his brother Neptune a lot. Jupiter helps me with everything I do including my art work, except that he doesn't come with me to the studio because he says Eighth Avenue has too much noise and traffic. He provides me with inspiration for many of my drawings and paintings, and like the magician he is, his presence in the art work assures its sale. He will usually sit in the chair next to me while I draw at home and walk on the paper if he doesn't approve. If I am away for longer than a few days he appears to me in my dreams and lets me know how he is. Jupiter is very inquisitive — a true seeker. He needs much sun and sleep to recharge enough to help me with all my business and also to help clean his brother Neptune. We try not to leave Neptune out, but sometimes it is hard because he is not very intelligent. We would like to be supportive to other artists and their cats.

Melissa Harris has a BFA in painting from Syracuse University and an MFA from Queens College. Her works have been included in solo and group exhibitions in New York, Syracuse and Paris. She has been the recipient of scholarships, fellowships and a Fulbright Travel Grant.

Magician's Helper, pastel and watercolor

MIRIAM JACOBS ❦

Crazy Face is my best friend. He waits for me by the door and is always there to comfort me. He hangs out with me while I make artwork and entertains the guests. I adopted Crazy when he was one to two years old. He had a difficult childhood, but after many years of psychotherapy he is stable — most of the time.

Crazy thinks about food a lot, although he is quite trim. He can get persistent about being fed and has bulimic tendencies. Mostly, he thinks he's a warrior. In spite of his advanced age of 13 years he still runs up and down and back and forth in my loft. At night Crazy stands guard at the end of my bed making sure no one comes and gets me.

For all this, I love Crazy Face dearly; I feed him and rough him up a bit, since boys like to be roughed up.

Miriam Jacobs has a BFA from SUNY, Buffalo, has received grants from Artists Space and Dance Theater Workshop and a scholarship from the Jerome Foundation. Her works have been included in solo and group exhibitions in New York, Boston, San Francisco and Berlin. She believes "that there is inherent in architectural forms an inner life." and it is her "purpose to explore this idea through photography and hand colored processes to literally draw out the essence of this belief."

The artist and Crazy Face

PHYLLIS JANTO 🐛

This is my Maine Coon cat, Feather, with her four-week-old kitten, The Great
Pumpkin, named for his color and size. Both are double-pawed; grumpy grandma
Elska decided not to sit for the family portrait. Also present is the midwife. Our cats
share our studio/home. Feather is good company, providing great entertainment
with her constant talking.

ESO

The artist with Feather and Pumpkin

*Phyllis Janto, a New York City sculptor, has a BFA and MFA from Hunter College and
Pratt Institute. She shows frequently in one-person and group exhibitions.*

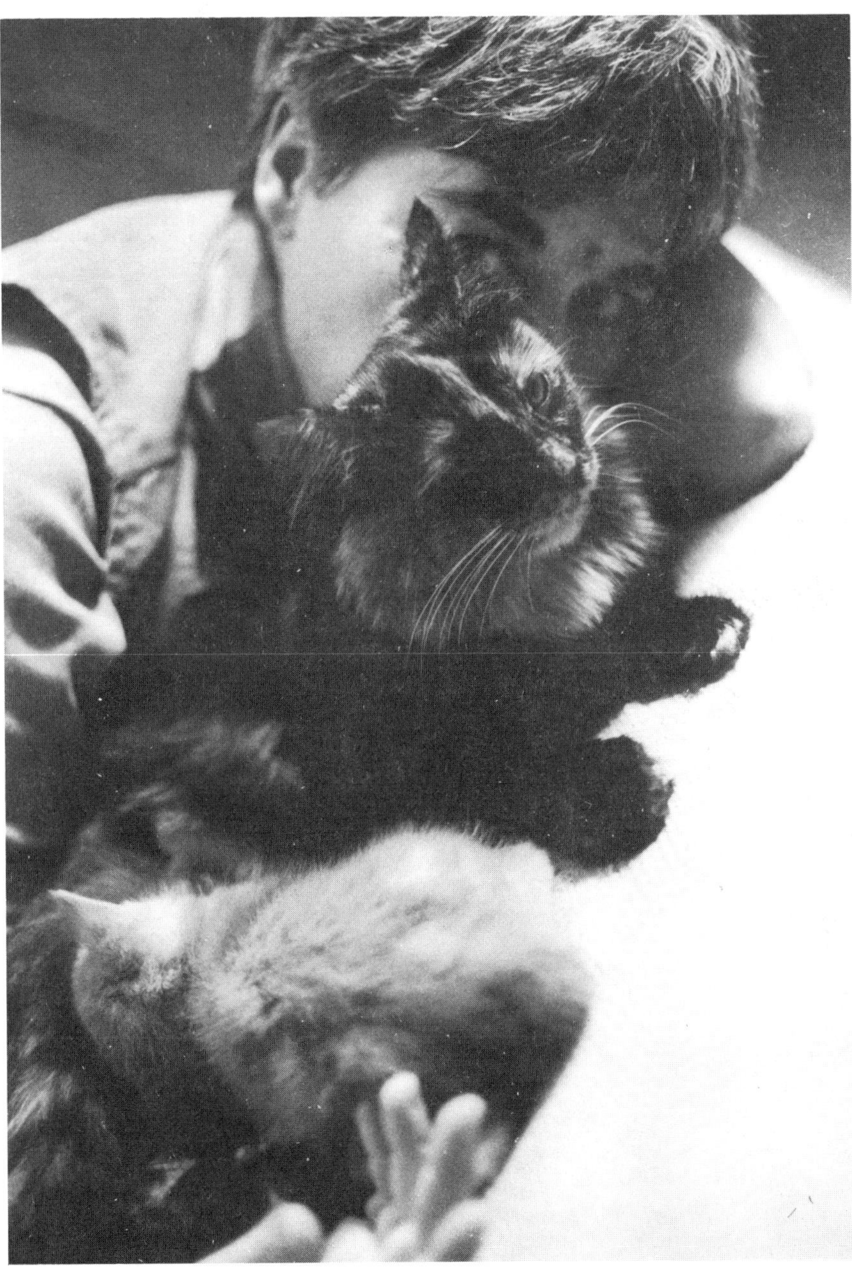

Phyllis Janto with Feather and Pumpkin

Tami Kander and Joe Lee 🍒

Mr. Black, cat, often (no, always) exhibits a keen artistic sensibility. Tami Kander, painter, cannot be found painting without his critical yowling and brush reaching. Failing these attempts at collaboration, Mr. Black goes paws on with the paper. The persistent artist makes his mark.

Emma, sensitive kitty, sings her praises to the arts. Sweet muse she is to Joe Lee, stirring the gentle musics of his soul. Ah, too soon the chorus halted with a bird in her smiling jaws.

Mr. Black and Tami Kander

Emma and Joe Lee

Tami Kander was born in Israel, educated in England and has lived in the United States since 1985. She is a painter, art therapist and a collector of vintage clothing.

Joe Lee, a native of Indiana, had a career as a circus clown traveling with tent shows. He quit that to work as a studio assistant in New York. Since moving back to Indiana, he has pursued a career as an art jeweler. He also writes and illustrates comic book stories for an underground press, Ripoff. He graduated from Indiana University.

Also, they have five cats.

Emma and Joe Lee

Mr. Black and Tami Kander

D. KLEINBEAST 🐾

This photo represents a highlight of an artist's experience. I was with the Rolls Royce of cats. I only wish this was my studio cat. I have the smaller model of the beast. Madam Vodi is 20 years old, grey and pink, and very much an opinionated studio cat. However, after my time with the tiger, I realized that the smaller pawed creatures carry within them 2,000 years of Siberian tiger blood. My cat doesn't sit for photos.

I love cats. Cats help to fire your imagination!

I recently lost Madam Vodi's mate of 15 years. Sir Plato was a classic Himalayan.

A recent note from D. Kleinbeast adds:

Unfortunately, since I last wrote to you, Madam Vodi passed on at 22. I am enclosing another Tiger Lady picture because I am the Tiger Lady and the photo hanging in my studio constantly gives me strength and fires my imagination. When you've been with the ultimate cat, a tiger, you understand William Blake. Incidentally, I have a new furry playmate, Royal Dutch Shana Pumium

D. Kleinbeast is a New York City sculptor enamored of big cats, but willing to compromise and accept small-sized ones for studio companions.

The artist, "Tiger Lady," with the real thing

DIANA KURZ 🐈

I have shared my home and studio with cats for over 30 years. I have often included them in my paintings and drawings, for their own sake, as cats, and for their intriguing shapes and forms. My pale calico Monette (named after Monet) is a pleasure and challenge to paint. There are no edges to the patterns and shapes of the colors of her long fur — she is not at all linear, like her shorter haired grey brother, Pema. I'm always happy when she decides to stay near me while I work, for I find her shy, gentle presence in my studio a delight, both for the aesthetic joy of looking at her and the distraction she affords.

Diana Kurz was born in Vienna and has lived most of her life in New York City. She received her MFA in painting from Columbia University. Kurz has exhibited widely in solo and group shows throughout the United States and France. Awards include a Fulbright Fellowship to France, a CAPS Grant from the New York State Council on the Arts, Yaddo and MacDowell Fellowships, and a one year American Center residency in Paris. In 1989, she showed her flower paintings at the Brooklyn Botanic Garden Gallery.

Monette and Diana Kurz

ARTHUR BYRON PHILLIPS 🐛

It was all because of my medium, egg-tempera, and my penuriousness. Unwilling to waste the egg whites and broken yolks, I put them aside in a bowl on my doorstep as a treat for passing creatures. One summer evening she was there, a tingling current of demonic caution. We began a friendship that continued for 12 years.

To human eyes she was not a handsome cat; nothing matched. Her fur was a confusion of colors, her tail was huge, her alabaster eyes were asymmetrical, the tiny body was an accidental result of Spring evenings with her consorts and the magic of kittens.

A cat-door was installed and she came and went, followed by her court, for the wheels of her family life revolved around her, the matriarch. Every February she would stalk into the frozen night to renew the genius for which she'd been born, and by April kittens were again hidden in the woodland that was her real home. Thus the court grew, kittens, cats and all her relatives sitting in my house through the night, all wild and untouchable, all to vanish with the morning dew. Bowls of cat food greeted their night calls, but food remained untouched until she arrived and ate her fill. The rest waited quietly until she'd finished and moved away.

I painted her many times, with all the pictures now in collections. In this, my last, I planned a painting of contrasts — the composition reflecting the fetal shape, the stone contrasting her softness. The urgent happiness of the kitten contrasted her patient anxiety, the nickel was her worth.

I touched her only twice — once when she was asleep — a touch greeted with a vicious attack. The second time she came to me, her eyes pleading for help. She was very old and very ill, and she permitted me to pick her up at last.

She remained in the house those last few days, watched over by me and her family. One last whispered message and she was dead. The valiant presence, the inspiration for creativity became a tiny fluff of matted fur.

I called to her family for months afterward, but they never returned; the gestalt was gone.

Armed with a BFA and MFA from the Pennsylvania Academy of Fine Arts and the University of Pennsylvania, Phillips took off for Paris, where he soon was doing portraits of notables such as Chanel, Colette, Dior and Helena Rubinstein. Determined not to be a formula painter, he spent two years in Florence experimenting with egg tempera, which became his life-long medium. Phillips's work is in major museums across the country, including the Cleveland Institute of Art, DeYoung Museum, Boston Fine Arts and the Brandywine Museum. He shows at Coe Kerr Gallery in New York.

Mrs. Crazy

HOWARDENA PINDELL

I am an artist and this is me with my big cat, Big Brother, who died several years ago at 14. He would sit for hours looking at my work, staring intently into the surface as if he had uncovered a vast universe. Big Brother was deaf so the visual was very important to him.

Howardena Pindell was born in Philadelphia. She earned her BFA at Boston University and MFA at Yale and is a professor of art at SUNY, Stony Brook. Pindell has been honored with numerous awards and fellowships, including two from the National Endowment for the Arts and the U.S. Japan Friendship Commission. Her work has been exhibited extensively throughout the United States, Africa and Europe and is in the collections of many major museums. Pindell has traveled to remote parts of Africa, the Caribbean, India, Japan, Brazil and northern and central Europe, studying universal spiritual traditions "as a link to understanding the culture" and "searching for alternative modes of living, thinking and seeing."

Howardena Pindell and Big Brother

LINDA PLOTKIN 🍒

Often, while I am arranging objects for my still-life paintings, Tina (short for Gatina) will wander in and arrange herself prominently in the composition. Occasionally she has been included in the final image, either as part of the composition, or, indirectly, when she walks across the surface of a wet watercolor, altering (and often improving) the pattern and texture.

Linda Plotkin, painter, lives and works in New York City, exhibiting at G.W. Einstein, Inc., Associated American Artists and Susan Teller Gallery. Her work is in the permanent collections of the Museum of Modern Art, the Brooklyn Museum and the Metropolitan Museum. In order to support her painting habit, Plotkin does free-lance work in voice-over narration.

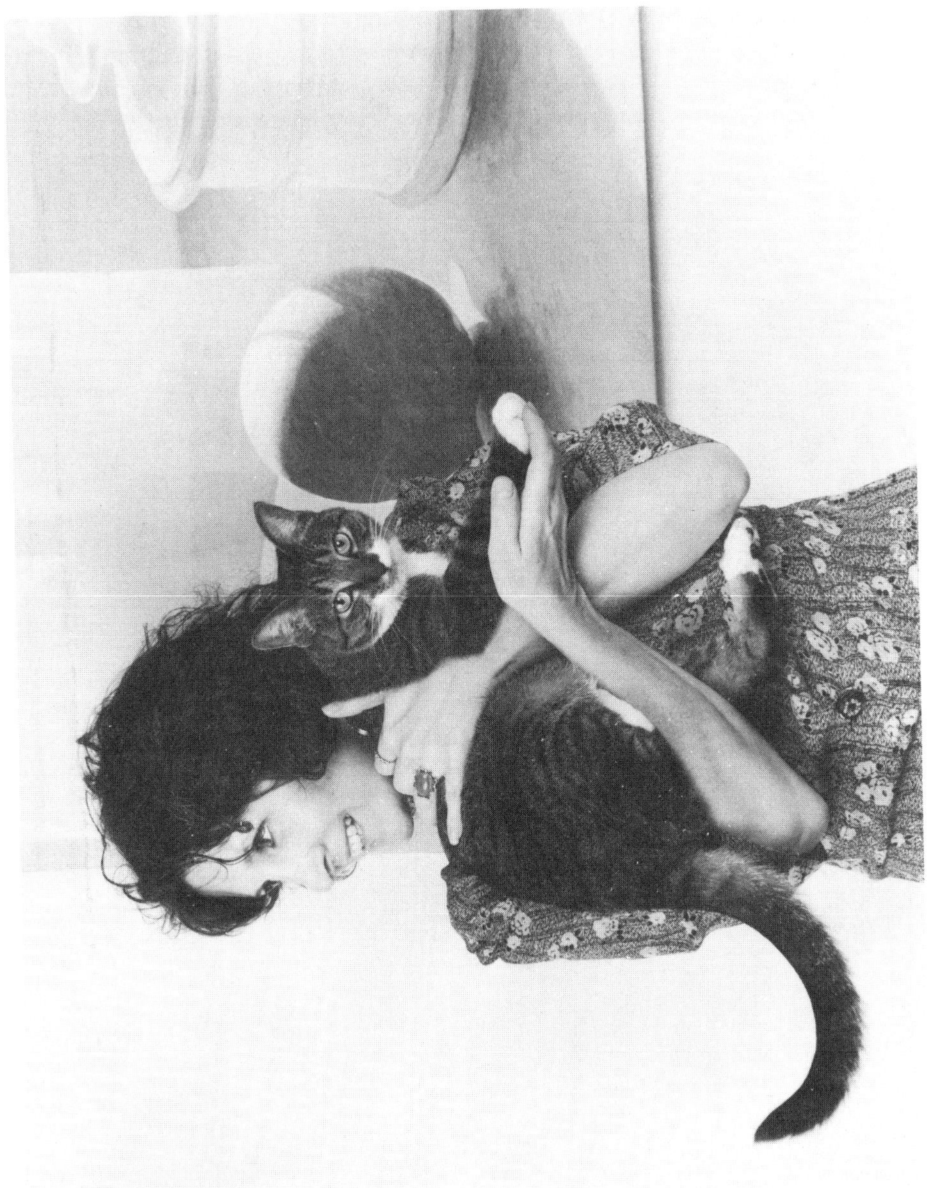

Linda Plotkin and Tina

MARGARET L. READ

Jinx is a male Persian, about 14 years old and very devoted to me. However, he is not a good model, since he always moves when he discovers I am painting him. He is a good "ratter," and old Charleston houses have many rats in their basements and in the walls, so Jinx has been invaluable for that. Not to mention that he is a great beauty, pure black with large amber eyes.

Margaret Read resides in a historic house on the Battery in Charleston, South Carolina, her native city, where she was educated, primarily, and where she works professionally. Having perfected her art form from studies throughout the United States, she is particularly noted for her paintings of cats, flowers and portraits.

SHELLEY RICE ❦

This is me and Chelsea (now deceased), the greatest cat on earth (or not), in 1984.
Chelsea was interested in all books, especially those in German.

Joan Greenfield

Shelley Rice and Chelsea

Shelley Rice is a writer, art critic, historian and author of Parisian Views.

CAROLEE SCHNEEMANN ❦

My cat is subject and muse in my work. He has been medium, joy and way of seeing since I crawled before walking and met the first one.

In *Cat Scan*, the death of a beloved companion cat leads to an investigation of cat images in Egyptian reliefs and friezes, as well as gestures and actions communicated directly from the cat in dreams and unexpected synergistic connection. Some of the ritualized gesture in my performance originated in a dream instruction from my cat, Cluny, after he unexpectedly died from a rat bite.

In one sequence of *Cat Scan*, "Look What the Cat Dragged In . . .," four readers compose sentences using "cat fragments" [phrases that enrich our language]: Cornered Cat, Cat's Paw, Sacred Cat, Eating Cats, Pussy is Pussy, Hell-Cats, Fat Cats, Copycat Deaths, Mangy Cat, Cat Killer, Copycat Suicides, Smelly Kitty Litter, Palestinian Tomcats, The Black Cat, Cat Box, Map of the Cat, A Cool Cat, Catcalls to Women, Cat and Mouse Game, Stray Cats, Wild Cat, Cat's Eye, Cat Scan, Nervous as a Cat, Cheshire Cat's Grin, Cat's Sense, Cattiness and Pettiness, Cat Carrier, Cat Food, Litters of Kittens, On the Catwalk, Skin a Cat, Starved Cat, Stray Kitten, Cat Stench, Cat Bites, Snarling Cat, Kittenish Girl, Catnip, Cat's Miaow, Pussy Lust, Cat Carcasses, Copy Cat Riots, Cat's Luck, Sissycat, Cat Nailed, Dead as a Cat.

In the photo series shown here, "Infinity Kisses" raises issues of "appropriate" eroticism. The intimacy between cat and woman becomes a refraction of the viewers' attitudes to self and nature, sexuality and control, the taboo and the sacred. My erotic film "Fuses" (1964) used the observant presence of our cat Kitch to establish parameters of a heterosexual diary which I filmed, even while participant. A subsequent diary film, "Kitch's Last Meal" (1973-76, double Super 8), examined daily life by tracking observations of the cat. The performance "Cooking With Apes" invited 18 cat participants (Stockholm 1973).

Since he was a kitten, my cat Cluny has awakened me every morning with deep kisses. Each week — even half asleep — I reach for a hand-held Olympus camera to film our kissing. Lighting, angles, exposure and focus are always unpredictable. Each resulting 35mm slide image is mirror printed in Xerochrome. These "flipped" images introduce permutations of repeated form as a time process, and the repeated rhythms of convexity, concavity eroticize the shapes surrounding the human and animal mouths.

continued on page 46

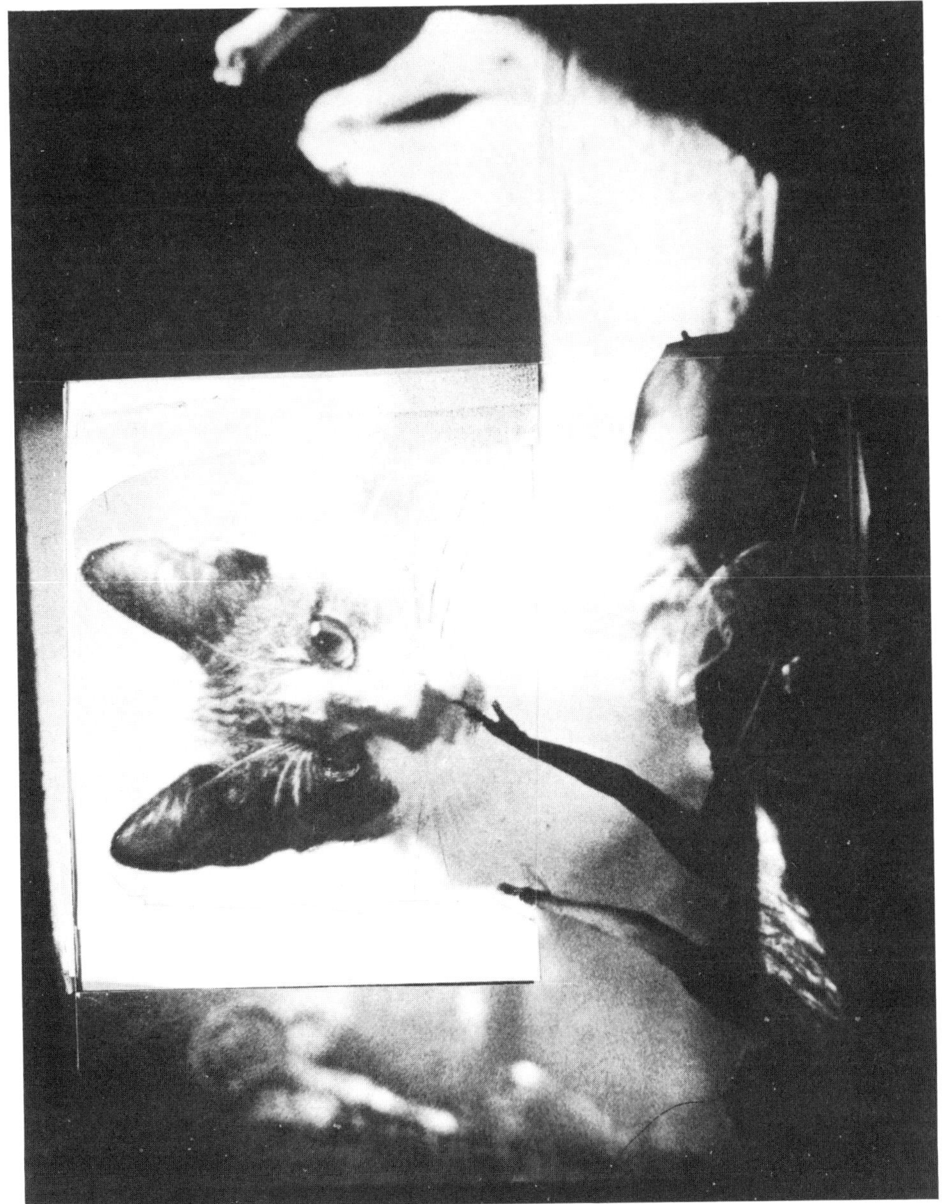

"Fresh Blood — A Dream Morphology," performance, 1985

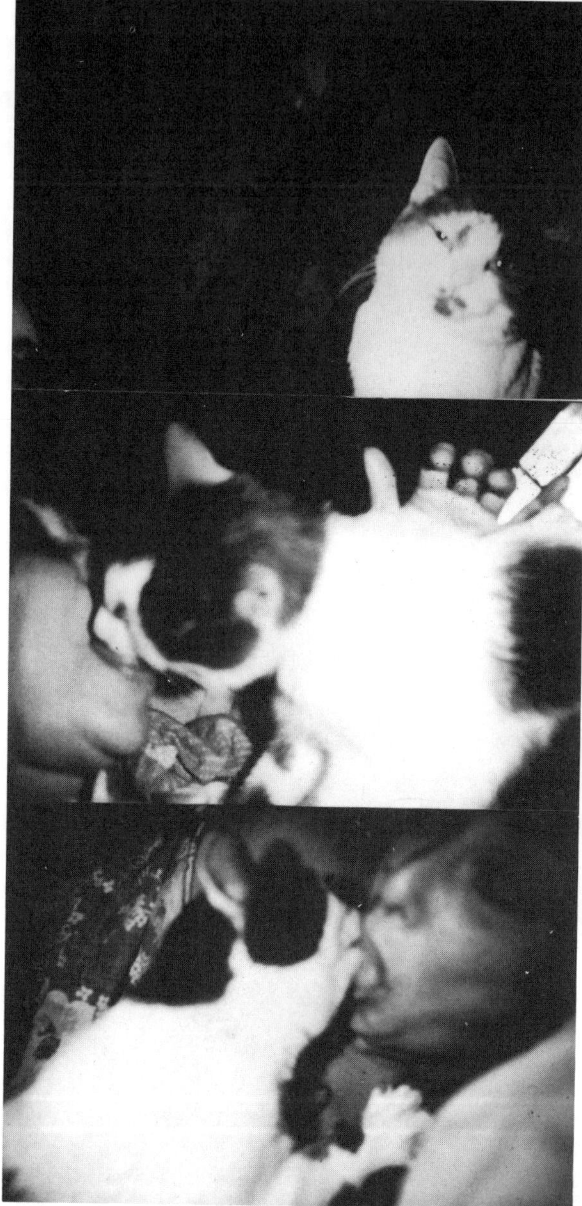

Cluny, 1981-87

Carolee Schneemann,
details from "Infinity
Kisses," 9'x12' wall,
120 units, 11"x17" each

Carolee Schneemann is a painter, performance artist, filmmaker and writer. Her work includes themes focusing on feminist history, the body as a source of knowledge, the integration of life with the art process and analysis of the cat's awareness.

46

ELFI SCHUSELKA and
DOMENICK CAPOBIANCO

When our cat Mezzanotte was very young, I'm ashamed to say that in a fit of sudden anger I kicked him several feet, where he landed and limped away favoring his right rear leg. I never kicked him again, but forever after and until his death every time I shouted at him in anger he would walk away with his right rear leg limping.

— *Elfi Schuselka*

Elfi Schuselka was born in Vienna and educated there at the Graphic and Experimental Institute (photography), the University of Vienna (Art History and Theater), Academy of Applied Arts and School of Vision, the Academy of Fine Arts, Naples, Italy; Art Students League and Pratt Graphics, New York. She teaches at CUNY, Baruch College, has won several international awards and has shown world-wide. Her works are included in several institutional and corporate collections. She lives and works in New York City.

So there I sat looking at a freshly stretched and primed and pristine white canvas on the wall, and next to me on the floor there sat our all-black, long-haired Maine Coon Cat Mezzanotte looking first at me then at the canvas and then back to me, etc., etc., etc., and after a while I left the studio, the canvas untouched, and in the morning when I returned, there on the canvas' lower right hand corner was a paw mark.

— D. Capobianco

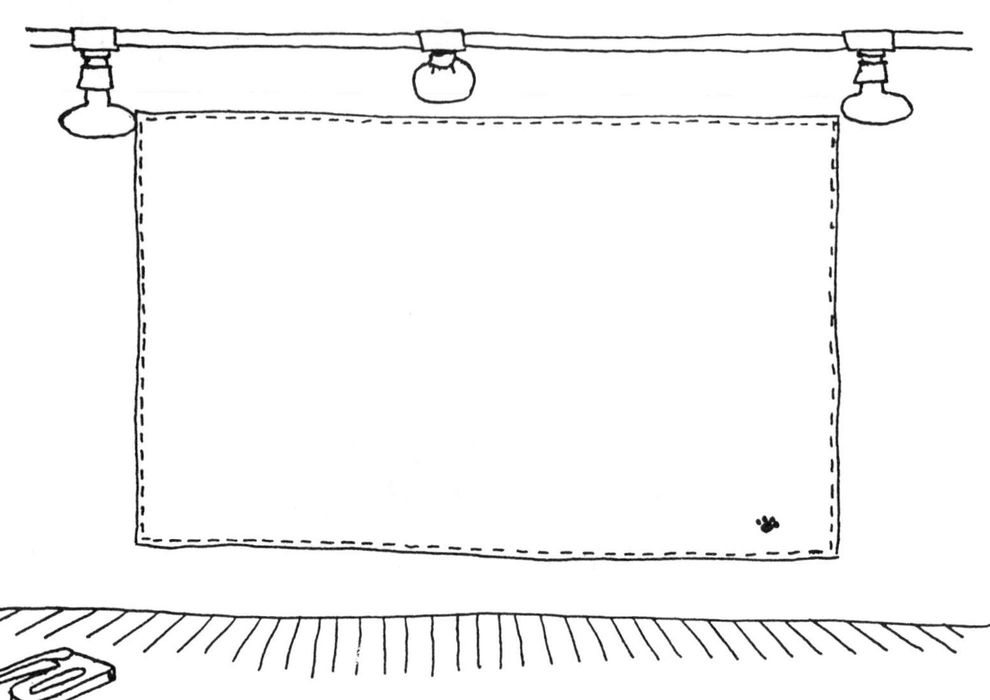

D. Capobianco received a BFA from Washington University, St. Louis, attended Skowhegan School of Painting and Sculpture and has been teaching at Rutgers University since 1967. He has been awarded six grants and fellowships, including a Guggenheim in 1984-85. His works have been in numerous solo exhibits and important international shows and are included in permanent collections in this country and abroad. He has illustrated book jackets, designed stage sets and published drawing portfolios.

RONALD STREET 🐾

My studio cat, Samurai, not only is a studio cat but a model, as you can see by the marble sculpture of him. Samurai can be found in many of my paintings and sculptures, but mostly he can be found asleep in the box containing my underwear.

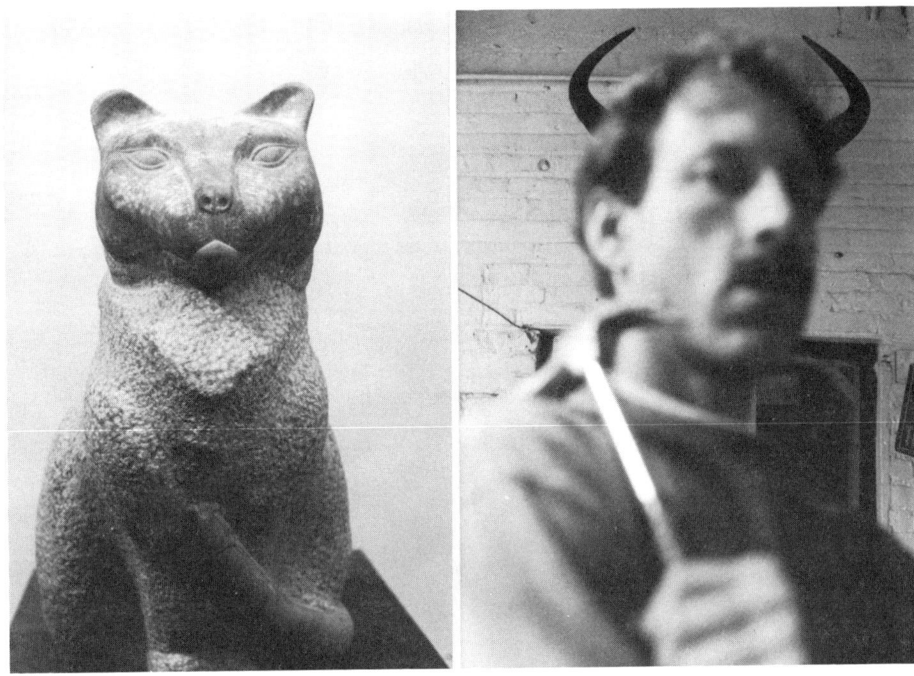

Samurai   Ron Street at Work

Ron Street, artist and master moldmaker at the Metropolitan Museum of Art, recently exhibited paintings in the Taft Museum's show "At the Table" and at City Without Walls' "Newark Through the Artists' Eyes." Street's sculptures are now on exhibition at La Paix Sculpture Garden and the Burlington College Sculpture Garden. Concurrently he is completing a commission from the Egyptian Government and the city of Memphis, Tennessee, to reproduce an exact copy of the 45-ton, 25-foot-high granite colossus of Rameses the Great.

VICTORIA VESNA 🍎

I did a number of works with the late White Boy, who was a very special cat, completely white, with one eye and deaf.
To me he immediately became a symbol of vulnerability of the spirit in the material world.
In 1984 I did a videotaped performance piece on the street, right after the Union Carbide disaster in Bhopal, India.
It coincided with the Christmas Holidays here.
We walked first through the Bowery, then Rockefeller Center.
The contrast of neighborhoods is amplified by the
contrast of the reactions of people.
White Boy, being deaf and in my arms, was quite content to walk around
amidst all the noise of buses, trucks, cars, people.
In fact, this special cat loved being involved in all the art projects,
even when I had to use glaring lights to shoot.

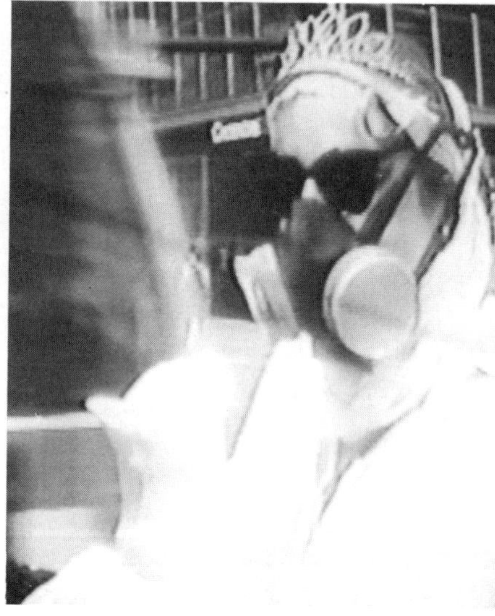

Detail from video "On the Street
with Bast" (9 min, NTSC,
color and B & W)

Victoria Vesna was born in Washington, D.C. and received a BFA from the University of Belgrade, Yugoslavia. She is a performance, film and video artist who has participated in several video festivals in Europe and performed in New York clubs, as well as in Germany and Yugoslavia.

Scene from "On the Street with Bast" (White Boy playing the role of Bast, Egyptian cat deity)

Janet Walsh 🍒

My helper is Simba, shown asleep on my easel. At the time, I lived and worked in my New York apartment.

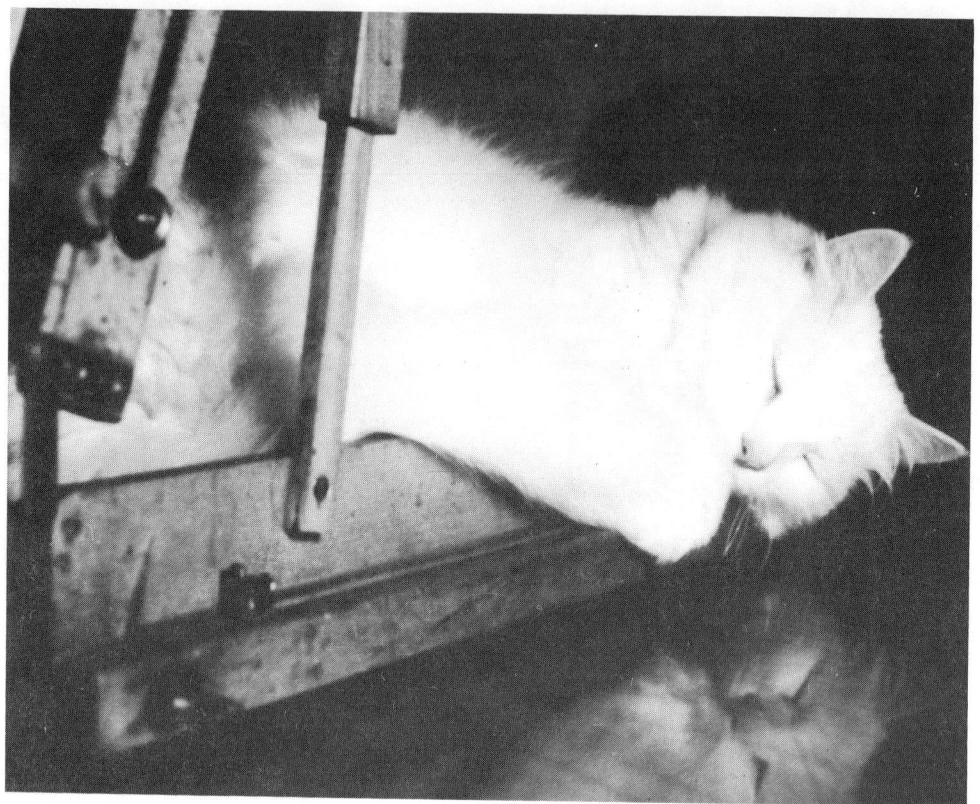

Simba, Art Critic

Janet Walsh lives and works in New York City and is a professional watercolorist.

52

F. Noreene Wells ❦

Elephi Pelephi well-known cat, formerly kitten, a cat of high i.q. is the full name (and also the title of a children's book) of my fifteen and a half-year-old orange and white foundling.

Elephi and his two equally flea-bitten, worm-infested siblings wound up under my rhododendron bush one nasty rainy October night. They were about eight weeks old, huddled together in the rain and crying piteously. Who could resist such a soggy mess? Homes were found for the sibs, and Elephi came to ground in the middle of five other cats, a very large black dog and a big house. The house, the dog and the five other cats are history — and Elephi is now senior cat in a two-cat household.

Elephi's Garden was done especially for a show at Gallery 10 Ltd. in Washington, D.C. Elephi is my subject quite often, but he hates the camera if it gets too close to him. I was working with both cats — Squire Cat, a grey striped tabby and pure photoham, simply disappeared in the grey striped world of the garden seen in black and white, so I began working with Elephi. I wanted something rather on the ominous side — sort of a "what creature is this lurking in the jungle?", but Elephi was not cooperating at all, so finally I yelled at him, which he hates. He halted and I snapped.

I love this photo. It's pure Elephi. And I love Elephi. Oh yes, and Squire Cat, too.

Noreene Wells grew up on a farm in Oregon with lots of cats, dogs, lambs, pigs, horses and monkeys. She attended a one-room schoolhouse until going off to college for degrees in zoology and bacteriology. She later studied photography at the Corcoran in Washington, D.C. and Glen Echo Park for the Arts. She says she is a generalist — working as artist and as free-lance photographer on assignments as well as videography.

Elephi's Garden

54

FAITH WILDING 🐈

"A cat can look at a queen."

Cats make ideal studio animals. They are completely observant and have total patience. They know when you need a little distraction, a little sensual stimulation. Pink tongue kisses. Playful bites on the ankle. An electrifying furry brush against the backs of your legs. Cats appreciate tools and materials, rustling paper, rolling and batting pencils, sucking brushes, and flicking up shreds of gold leaf with tiny pink tongue-tips. Cats have a life of their own, and they are willing to live it alongside of you. They'll tolerate, but never beg for, your foolish needy need to love and touch and talk silly baby talk. Cats never lose face, and they help you regain yours.

(In memory of two beloved studio cats, Bianca and Miú.)

Faith Wilding is an artist who paints, draws, writes and works in radio. She is a member of the Heresies Collective, lives in New York City, and teaches part-time at Cooper Union.

Lori Valesko

Faith Wilding and Bianca, 1980

56

ABBIE ZABAR

Timothy spends a lot of his time asleep in a favorite laundry basket. Or on a hot summer day, he prefers taking his naps next to the cool base of a toilet bowl.

But during the times that we work together he can be walking across my collages with the very piece of paper that I need hanging from his tail, sitting under the very bush that I've decided to prune, or doing his grooming right on the very galleys and manuscripts that I am reviewing.

In fact, it's not for nothing that he was prominently thanked in the acknowledgements of my little book, *The Potted Herb*. . . . "Plus an extra tin of tuna for Timothy, who much to both my delight and annoyance, always managed to stay on top of things."

Timothy working

Abbie Zabar, a native New Yorker, is an artist, writer, co-founder and artistic director for E.A.T., a gourmet specialty store in New York, and when all else fails, a gardener. She lives and works with a furry grey cat named Timothy.

MARTIE ZELT

I did this woodcut for my graduating "wall" at the Pennsylvania Academy of Fine Arts in 1954. The actual work was printed on Japanese troya paper in sections; the approximate total size was three and a half feet high by four feet wide. I no longer have any impressions of the woodcut, since my life after that year took me to far places. I still have lots of cats. One lived to be nineteen and a half.

Women and Cats, 1954

Martie Zelt attended Temple University in Philadelphia as well as the Pennsylvania Academy. She lives in Bristol, Virginia. Her style has gradually become abstract, but she is still doing prints and showing them in one-person and group exhibitions. Zelt has been honored with several purchase awards and her works are included in the collections of the Brooklyn Museum, Carnegie Institute, and Princeton and Yale Universities, among others.